There is a hedgehog house next to the wall in the garden. A family of hedgehogs lives in it.

1

There is a little tunnel in the wall for the mother hedgehog to get in and out of the garden.

One day Jelly and Bean see the little hedgehogs by the wall. They are looking very sad.

The mother hedgehog is missing. She went out of the garden and she has not come back.

Jelly and Bean go to look in the tunnel. A ball is stuck in it. The mother hedgehog cannot get back.

Jelly goes into the tunnel. She pushes the ball until it falls out of the tunnel at the other end.

The mother hedgehog is waiting. She pushes the ball away. Then she climbs into the tunnel.

Soon she is back in the garden and the family of hedghogs are all together again.